How I Wrote My First Novel

My steps, pitfalls, and revelation as a wife and mother

Treviance Mayo

How I wrote my first Novel/My steps, pitfalls, and revelation as a wife and mother

ISBN-13:
978-0692870402 (Mayo Media Inc.)

ISBN-10:
0692870407

Copyright© 2017 by Treviance Mayo

Cover design and cover photo by Mayo Media Inc.

Published by Mayo Media Inc.

Contact: Mayomedia@live.com

MAYO MEDIA

DEDICATION

To all who dream to become an author,
it's never too late...

ACKNOWLEDGMENTS

Thank you to my Beautiful Godhead; God the Father, God the Son- our savior Jesus Christ, and God the Holy Spirit!

My wonderful husband, advisor, teacher and business partner, Ronald Mayo. I love you babe!

My four beautiful children, Ci-Ci, Ronnie, Jordan, and Ahlia, who keep me grounded

My late mother Kathryn Mae Gholson, who always got on me about reading my bible.

My friends and family for their prayers and continued support.

Prayer

Father in the name of Jesus, I pray that every person who reads this book will be encouraged to seek you first so that you will guide them along as they go on their journey of their God given destiny as authors for You. I pray that you will impart into them a longing to get to know you better and a will to finish every book that you give them to write. Thank you, Lord. Amen.

Contents

Introduction

Hello friend! If you're reading this book, then you are either thinking about writing your first novel, just getting started, or maybe even started a long time ago, but never finished. Keep going! This book is a sneak peek into my process. It is not a course in writing. Writing is a journey unto itself.

Allow me to introduce myself. My name is Tre.' I'm 1st and

foremost a lover of God. God the Father, God our savior Jesus Christ and God the Holy Spirit. Personally, one of the names I like to refer to Him is my Beautiful Triune God. He has blessed me with a wonderful husband, 4 children, and two bonus children.

In this book, I will include why I decided to become an author, how I found time to create while being a busy wife and mother, my experience with choosing the right tools for me, and the steps I took to finish and publish my novel. Why?

Because I would like to inspire others who are starting their journey, or struggling to finish. It's not an easy task. My heart goes out to those who dream of becoming an author. I know what it feels like. We must pray that God will give us a guidance or a push along the way. On my journey of writing, I have taken the time to read other people's experiences. Whether it was positive or negative, it helped me to push forward through the rough times.

Here are my personal steps, my perspective...My story.

Chapter 1

I finally finished my book!

Sooooo, I had finally finished my first book.

Something I never thought I would do. If I could have had it my way, I would just keep editing it for the rest of my life until it was perrrrfect. The problem was that it would never be perfect in my eyes. An awesome individual from my writers group helped me to come to the realization of the fact that as my life changes with time and so will my ideas, so I finally independently published it.

Where did my love for writing begin?

It was a normal day in elementary school. I was a ten-year-old with long dark brown pigtails. I was tall for my age with a big imagination. Fifth grade was an interesting year for me. It was the first time that my school was holding a thousand word writing contest. I was super excited to have a chance at winning. Our work would be judged by length, creativity, and accuracy. I couldn't wait to get home and tell my mom all about it.

I excitedly jumped off the school bus and ran into the house to announce the good news. Being a single mother of five, she was always busy. Although she was in the middle of her duties, she stopped and smiled, cheering me on.

I was the type of child that was always making up little stories to act out with my siblings. We would use whatever we could find and incorporate it into our act; from paper characters that we drew, to baby dolls. It didn't matter. We always knew how to stay entertained.

I hugged my mom and ran to my bedroom. I felt a surge of energy burst through my body and happily began my journey of creative writing. We had two weeks to submit our work. At the time, I loved horror stories. When finished, I titled it, *The Scary House*. I'd never had any training other than my reading and writing classes, but I was determined to win. I nervously turned it in. Each day after that seemed longer than the prior.

After a month of anticipation...finally!

The day had arrived and the winner would be announced.

My teacher smiled at us. "Okay everyone, before we present the winner, I'm going to pass out some books."

My teacher handed all of the participants a newly printed hardback book. I was next. I had to do a double take. She had surprised us with a copy of our work. My eyes widened in shock and I could hear my heart pounding as I gazed at my very own designs! My words! To me, it was my best-selling novel!

Even though I didn't win the trophy, I thought, *Who cares.* I was so pleased with my work that my grand prize was in my hands! I took it home and wooed my family, soaking up all the praises.

Weeks later, my Mom received a letter in the mail. It was from my school, letting her know that they saw potential in me. I was qualified to join a special program for young writers. Unfortunately, there were no grants available for this and my Mom lovingly explained that we couldn't afford it. I pretended to be okay but my little heart was broken. How was I to become an author if I couldn't get the proper training?

As time went on, I realized that I also had a love for music. By age eleven I started writing songs. I teamed up with some cousins and we had a ball singing and harmonizing to original lyrics. I went on to join everything I had access to; chorus, band, modeling, female trios, and acting. Entertainment became the thing that excited me. The thing that I knew I would do for the rest of my life.

Years later, I'm all grown up and feeling something inside my heart, tugging at me to write again. I thought to myself, "*Why in the world did I wait until I was married with children? Why pursue my dream of becoming an author after so many years had passed?"* I could hear that little girl inside of me saying, "It's never too late." I had finally decided to write a book in the year 2007.

Because I'm a lover of fiction, I created my first Christian romance/suspense novel titled, _Fancee/ A rose amongst thorns._

Why romance /suspense? Since I had accomplished nine years of marriage at the time, I felt that I should write about something that I was seasoned in.

In the first few years, my husband and I were in a place where we were trying to sort it all out, from communication problems, to organization issues, temptations, people trying anything and everything to separate us, and on top of that… baby mamma drama, and raising small children. Everything that a couple could possibly have to deal with...that was us.

I did a lot of praying and researching. It

was either that or give up. I had never been married before, so during my research, I began to wonder, "What was the norm? What were other couples going through? How did they deal with disagreements?"

So many questions entered my mind. I decided to interview Christian couples that were together, separated, and divorced. You name the situation, I interviewed it. I took lots of notes. Being able to see other perspectives helped my marriage and my creative process.

I took a few college courses in advanced writing and finished my novel in 2014, but there was still something missing. Sometimes you may need to reach out to people for guidance. There's always someone out there that has already done what you are trying to do.

When I first started reaching out, it was hard because I knew that not everybody was my friend.

Be careful of who you deal with. People will do mean things; use you, take your ideas, talk about you behind your back, and the list goes on.

The good thing is if we pray and ask God for help, He will give us favor with people who will guide us to people who will share secrets of their success and push us into the right direction. They will be our personal cheerleaders. Sometimes that's all we need in order to keep pushing forward.

One of my favorite memorized scriptures that builds my faith is:

[7] Ask, and it shall be given you; seek, and ye shall find; knock, and it shall be opened unto you: [8] For every one that asketh receiveth; and he that seeketh findeth; and to him that knocketh it shall be opened. (Matthew 7:7-8 KJV)

I was blessed with three mentors to guide and inspire me to finish my novel. I tell you; it was not easy. They did not do the work for me. They pointed me in the right direction.

It was either (A) learn it myself and invest some money, or (B) pay lots of money for someone else to do it all for me. Of course, I chose (A).

I also joined a local writer's group. At first, I was a little biased at attending because I didn't have a personal relationship with the members. I would show up and listen instead of sharing.

The more I listened to other people's process of writing and ideas, the easier it became for me to share. My skills improved and I started asking the right questions that helped me along my journey.

I published "Fancee" a Christian romance suspense novel in October of 2016.

So...are you wondering how in the world I found time to complete a full novel?

Okay, keep reading!!

Chapter 2

Who has time to write a book?

Before I started my journey to create my first novel, I would often hear, "Who has time to write a book?"

In this day and age, we are living in a world of advanced technology. It's hard to find time to write, especially if you have even a part time job, a spouse and lots of energetic children who love spending time with you. Not to mention helping the kids with their homework, cooking, cleaning, and the list goes on and on and on. Here's the thing: If you love to write, make sure you don't treat it like a chore. I like to treat it as a getaway after I've organized and accomplished my other duties, and sometimes a breath of fresh air while I'm taking a break.

I'll share a few tips that helped me:

- Invite God to this event. Ask Him for wisdom, knowledge, understanding and revelation. Ask the Lord to show you what route to take and give you ideas.
- Create a private place in your Home that fits the type of environment that you like to write in.
- Take a voice recorder everywhere you go and voice record ideas.
- Have a balanced schedule.
- Be sure to communicate.
- Choose the right time of day that fits your situation.
- Just go for it!!

Create a place in your home that nobody can use but you. This is where you keep all of the material things that spark your creativity; sticky notes, posters, books. Anything and everything that will help to get you going.

Take a voice recorder everywhere you go, just in case you have an idea, but no time to write (I use my cell phone).

Have a balanced schedule. For example: Work, chores, spending time with the family, exercising, writing, relaxing, and other tasks that are important to you. Also, pin it up on the wall so that your whole family can see. It may take a while to master it, but you will if you're persistent.

Be sure to communicate with everyone when you're about to go into writing mode. I find that my family has to be reminded. Ask if there's anything they need before you start. Let them know what time you'll be available. Put a sign on the door, "Do not disturb unless there's an emergency." Now that my children are older, I find that this method works for me. My family respects me when I'm specific.

I've had plenty of days where my husband may have been working late and was not available to keep an eye on the children (when they were younger). If that's your situation or if you're a single parent with small children, you may have to choose a time of the day when your kids are asleep. For example, early in the morning or late at night. The tricky part to this method is getting enough sleep so that you will be sharp the next day. According to Jeffery Jones from Gallup.com, experts say that we need about eight hours per night, but the national average is less than seven.

If you find yourself procrastinating, go into spiritual warfare against it! Command procrastination, slumber and sleepiness to go in Jesus name. After you pray, in faith, just start writing! Always pray before you do anything. Other ways to drum up creativity after praying is to watch a movie or read a book. Go work out at the gym or listen to a motivational speaker. Do something different every time. God will also use these types of activities to spark your creativity. I remember getting writer' s block. It lasted for a few days. After praying, engaging in activities with my family and giving my frustrations to God, ideas started pouring in again and I was back to my getaway!

You can do this!

Chapter 3

My writing process from start to finish

I. I Selected a genre

There are many genres to choose from. Sometimes it's easier to wait until your work is finished to decide which one your story falls into. I started out with women's fiction and after the final draft, I realized that Christian romance/suspense was a better fit.

II. Characters

1. I created my main characters in the beginning. From there, I added

characters when needed.

2. I created a profile for each character (name, age, socioeconomic status), what does he/she have to accomplish or overcome? What does he/she want? What will be their development throughout the story?

III. I wrote an outline

1. Kept an open mind, knowing that my outline could change at any time.
2. Gave a short analysis of what happened in each chapter.
3. Asked myself, "What are the primary issues in the story?"
4. Organized events that brought cause and effect.

IV. Begin your journey of writing the first draft! Here's what I did:

1. Experimented with the characters, styles, and plots.
2. Researched technical parts of the book. For instance, if a character was at a hospital getting treated for a gunshot wound, I would look up the correct terms that doctors and nurses would use in that type of situation.
3. Write, write, write, and oh yeah...WRITE!!! Even if it's just one page per day, I made sure I accomplished it.
4. I read it out loud as I wrote the dialogue.
5. If there was a scene in the book that bothered me, I'd skip it. I would get back to it when it was time to rewrite. Some of the scenes in my novel irked me. When it came time to rewrite, I realized they didn't belong

there in the first place.

6. Don't edit yet. I find that I move a lot faster if I focus solely on creating first. How do I know? Trial and error. The first half of my book took the longest because I was so worried about misspelled words, punctuation, rewriting whole chapters; and the list of errors go on and on. One of my mentors had to explain to me that I was putting too much stress into my writing process. You must resist the urge to edit while creating. This is helpful, especially for the newbies!! Many of my friends have confessed to me that they were so bogged down with focusing on their mistakes, that they just gave up.

7. I followed my outline and kept going until the rough draft was finished.
This helped me to have a smooth flow of writing.

V. Take a break, then revise!

Once my rough draft was done, I had to step away and focus on other things for a few months. I did this because I needed to be able to look at my work with a fresh pair of eyes. You don't have to wait as long as I did. Just a few days could help.

VI. When I was ready to give it another go, I had to ask myself a few questions…

1. Is it going at a good steady pace? Too fast? Too slow?
2. Are there any holes in my plot? Is it making sense?
3. Are my details accurate?

4. Are the characters relatable? Are they believable?

5. Am I using the correct structure for the genre I chose?
6. Does the story move me?
7. Is it a good read?

These questions provoked me to do a re-write and revise until I was happy with my work.

VII. Time to edit! Okayeee…editing can drive you bonkers! Here are steps I took.

1. I went over my work, correcting every error I could find, and reading it out loud to myself and others. It helps in a major way. If you find yourself having a hard time reading it out loud, chances are you need to make a correction in that area.
2. I connected with a mentor who had experience in writing books to get advice.

3. I copyrighted my novel with the Library of Congress.

According to the <u>US Copyright office</u>, you can copyright your work online. They will instruct you to go to <u>Copyright.gov/eco</u> and follow these steps:

A. Click "Login to eCO."

B. Click "If you are a new user, click here to register."

C. Fill out the form and click "Next."

D. Complete setup of your copyright office account.

E. Go back to the above website and click "Login to eCO" again.

F. Follow the steps to file a copyright for your book. Books are filed   as "Literary Work".

4. I paid a professional to go over my work. I was too emotionally attached to do it all myself. Because I chose to get outside help, I now understand a lot more about editing than I ever did before. Luckily, I found a private editor who worked with me on pricing and taught me the different steps to take. Here are four types of editing that was used for my novel.

- Content editing
- Line editing
- Copy editing
- Proofreading

1. Content editing- Checking the content for factual errors, contradictions, and inconsistencies. After my editor did this,

I rewrote sections and improved the quality of the text.

2. Line editing removes every unnecessary word, going over it line by line. This type of editing is sometimes combined with content editing.

3. Copy editing checks the language of the text; spelling, grammar, syntax, and other mechanical problems

4. Proofreading is when you do a light copy edit as you are looking over the book. This is after it is laid out in the format in which it will be printed.

Note: If you can't afford to pay for professional help, maybe ask a friend who has an English major. I asked friends to review my novel.

Here' s a word of advice, only ask friends that will tell you the truth. This is important. It may compel you to change something before you publish it.

Chapter 4

Will you be happy with your novel twenty years from now?

When I first started writing my novel, I was not happy. I knew that if I wouldn't have sought and found the help I needed, I would have never been satisfied. I wouldn't have published it. I've learned that zealousness will get you nowhere. I had to practice patience and push for quality.

I realize that my work is not only for the

readers out there in the world, but it's for me. If I'm not moved by what I write, why even put it out?

In my opinion, when you believe in your creation, people will draw to it because they want to know why you believe in it.
Is it a life lesson?
Will it keep their attention?
Will it help them?
People want to know how your work is benefiting you, and if it can benefit them as well. I always ask myself this challenging question:

Will I be happy with my work twenty years from now? (If my answer is **no** then I have more work to do.)

Chapter 5

Your cover is the first impression!

Your cover can make or break your book. I've had several customers tell me that the cover alone provoked them to purchase my novel. A good cover should have these types of qualities:

1. Catch eyeballs!
2. Emotionally connect with people.
3. Intellectually connect to the reader.
4. Have a message in itself.

I waited until my novel was finished to design the cover. Because I plan to adapt my novel into a feature film, I decided to cast a real person as the main character, "Fancee." I teamed up with my husband and daughter, and we had a photoshoot. I put a lot of thought into what her facial expression would be, because it had to exude a woman with problems to face. She's surrounded by beautiful roses, and there is a mystery man positioned behind her, far off into the distance. He's watching and waiting. Together we formed a masterpiece that complimented the storyline.

People who have purchased my novel tell me that when looking at the cover, they wonder, is the man stalking her? Is he her husband? A friend? The look in Fancee's eyes gives off a sense of mystery, which provokes them to ask, "What's her story?"

In designing my cover, I asked myself, "What is it saying to the reader? What about the book is important to me?"

I had to convey the answers to these questions on the cover. If it doesn't have a message then it's not worth checking out.

Note: If a reader is not impressed with your cover, they might skip pass your masterpiece and miss out on a good read.

Chapter 6

My favorite tools

I like to use several different tools all at the same time.

Why??

Earlier, I shared my first time writing as a fifth grader. I wrote a thousand words by hand. We didn't have a computer or typewriter at the time.

As an adult, I got my first laptop and installed Microsoft word on it. This was the only tool I used. The learning process was hard for me. Once I started getting proficient at it, I was on a role until one horrible day. Nothing could prepare me for what was about to happen. I got to chapter eight of my first novel and BAM!!! I accidently erased everything. It automatically saved and I could not get it back. Still new to the program, I had no idea what to do to resolve my dilemma. I thought about quitting. As a matter of fact, I did for a few months. I focused on other things. My irritation lingered on like a nagging cough. Eight chapters is a lot to a new author. With my busy schedule, it had taken so long to get that far. The reality of the matter is that I had to make a choice. Was my love for writing strong enough to start all over again?

YES!!!

Eventually I got back to my hide away,

but from that point on, I vowed to always save my ongoing work on multiple programs.

Here are my favorite tools:
- Microsoft word
- My cell phone
- A USB thumb drive
- Google docs
- Scrivener

Yes, I do…I use them all. One might think its overkill, but I'd rather have peace of mind than lose something that I've put a lot of time and energy into.

Microsoft word has templates to choose from or you can just manually format your novel.

Thumb drive/Sim card in Cell phone: Send yourself a copy of your work and save it on your cell phone or stick a thumb drive in your computer and save. I always do this as a backup. So many things can happen; House fire and theft are just two examples of a long list of possibilities.

Google Docs: My favorite reason for using Google docs is that I can invite people to read my work without going through too many hoops. I can also choose to make it unavailable when finished. You can open it up from any computer as long as you have Wi-Fi, and it saves as you go. You can learn more by going to the G suite learning Center by Google. This is where you can find instructions on how to use it. Also, it's being saved in a location other than home, which provides even more protection.

Scrivener: This tool is my all-time favorite. According to the maker of this program,

Literature and Latte, it's a word processor and project management tool created specifically for writers of long texts such as novels, screenplays, and more. It has templates. It combines all the tools you use for writing in one application and saves your work for you. It's available for Mac or Windows. One of my favorite reasons for using Scrivener is that I can save it in the different formats I need when publishing my book, such as Mobi, PDF, rich text, plain text, word, e-pub, and .html, just to name a few. I went through a major learning curve, but it's so worth it. Here is a link from the _Literature and Latte_ website. It will give you an overview of this awesome program:

https://www.literatureandlatte.com/video.php

Now...if one tool fails, you'll have many backups my friend!

Chapter 7

My publishing experience

I had just finished my final adjustments and was ready to publish. By this time, I had done a lot of research on whether I wanted traditional or self-publishing.

"…publishing is a branch of a culture and production that involves the preparation and distribution of books, magazines, newspapers, and graphic material."- Farlex Free Dictionary.

Traditional publishing is when a publishing

house buys the rights to your work. They put up the money needed to market and distribute a finished version of your book. Depending on the contract, the author could receive an advance on future royalties. The downside of this is that it can take years of submitting your manuscript to publishing houses before it is picked up and published.

Self-publishing is when **you** pay for everything needed to publish your book; professional editing services, marketing, distributing, and the list goes on. I choose self-publishing for my books mainly because I wanted full, creative control over content and design, and higher royalties of course. It's an empowering experience.

I published my work through Amazon/KPD, Nook, iBooks and Kobo. Being that it was my first time, it was definitely a learning experience. Luckily, Scrivener allows me to save in the formats that I need to publish my book. I used Microsoft word for my PDF files.

Here are the file formats I used for each company.

- Amazon for digital – Mobi (Scrivener)
- Kindle direct publishing – PDF (I used a KPD- template in Microsoft word and saved it in PDF format for paperback)
- Nook – epub (Scrivener and PDF for the paperback version)
- iBooks – epub (Scrivener)
- Kobo – epub (Scrivener)

I used scrivener to create the mobi file for Amazon. Also, once you upload it, Amazon will automatically point out some of the errors that you might have missed.

Kindle direct publishing will provide a template

based on the size and page count of your book for free. If you don't like their template, there are plenty of online sites that you can choose from that may have what you're looking for. Just google, "book templates". I used the KDP template with Microsoft word.

Nook accepts epub format, in which I used Scrivener. I used a PDF file for the paperback version.

iBooks and Kobo accepts epub format. I used Scrivener for these companies as well. Each company is slightly different when it comes to the file size of the photos.

I chose to save money and do it myself. This was a challenging learning curve. Even though self-publishing companies give you step by step instructions, you still have to know how to put your book in the correct format, and have the time and patience to trouble shoot when problems arise. It can be rather frustrating. Anytime that I felt stuck, I would stop, take a breath, read the instructions again, ask around, find youtube self-help videos, and do more research. Once I got it right, I was relieved to finally have published my first book.

Well, it didn't stop there. I would like to share something with you that is one of the most frustrating things that self-publishing authors deal with.

Finding small mistakes after you' ve published your work!!!!!

When you find small mistakes, it can make your blood boil, and your skin crawl! This is true...especially after you' ve already had a professional go over it, and you've spent countless hours of proof reading. No matter how good your editor is, it happens.

The good news is that Amazon, Nook, Kobo, iBooks, and other companies have made it possible to make corrections, even after you've published your book! Yay!

I was so happy to discover this. It was still irritating to have to go back and republish, but it's worth it, especially if those small missed errors bother you.

Most of the self-publishing authors that I spoke to hired professionals to put their books in the proper format, and publish it for them. If you do this, be sure to research the company and beware of scams.

Would I accept a publishing deal?

If I was offered a traditional publishing deal for the right terms, and conditions, I would definitely consider taking it.

Currently, I choose not to. Out of obedience to God, I choose to get my books out into readers' hands right away in the digital outlets and physical stores that the Lord leads me to publish them in.

Chapter 8

Let's Party!

I had finally published my masterpiece! A fiction book titled: *Fancee*. The only thing I could think of at the time was parrrrtaaaaay! Some may think that it's easy to plan a party. Nope! I cannot stress enough that in order for people to take you seriously, you have to invest time and money into yourself. On this journey, I've learned that with professionalism, you will gain respect, and lots of support.

We scheduled the celebration one month out and ordered all the promotional material that we needed to pull it off; Posters, business cards, invitations, a retractable banner, book marks, the paperback versions of my novel, and more. We made a list of all that we needed and stayed organized.

Another thing that is important is food. We made sure that we knew ahead of time what type of food to serve and locked in volunteers to assist. If you take care of your guests, they will tell lots of people about your awesome hospitality and professionalism. They will buy your book!

Was this expensive?

Yes!

We spent our hard-earned money to make it happen. Here's the thing…we felt good about it. The only thing that mattered on this special day was that we had lots of fun celebrating my baby! My masterpiece that I've been working on for years is finally released to the world!!!

Here's a checklist we used for our celebration:

- o Marketing materials (poster, bookmarks, banner, business cards, invitations)

- o Decorations

- o Food/Drinks (including table cloths, dishes, and utensils)

- o Games

- o Clothing

- o Volunteers

- o Prizes

- o Venue

- o List of invites

o Music

o Paperback books and marker or pen for signing

o Petty cash and a credit card reader

o We made sure to lock down the venue, and order my paperback books and marketing materials early to allow ample time for delivery.

o We invited our guests three weeks ahead of time through social media sites, and sent out a few reminders close to the date. We also printed out invitations for those who were not on social media.

o We ordered the food and prepared prizes a week ahead of time. We also picked out a list of songs to play in the background, and had a video trailer for my book, repeating on a big screen.

o We decorated the venue the day before and made sure all of our I's were dotted and T's crossed.

o One of the tricky parts of this experience was picking out what games to play. My love for acting inspired me to create a game. I called it, "Scripted". I chose two volunteers from the audience and handed them a script from my novel. They were challenged to act out the scenes. It was a win/win. The volunteers gained prizes, and the crowd was entertained. Some people admitted that this game rekindled their passion for acting.

o The second game was my version of

"The Paperback Game."

Dwight Garner's version that he put out in his New York Times article was one that peeked my interest, so I decided to change it a little. I handed the players a sheet of paper and pencil. I then had a volunteer read the blurb from the back of my book and gave the players two minutes to write down what they thought the first sentence of the first chapter of my novel would be. After the two minutes were up, each player read their version out loud. The one who's first sentence was the closest won the prize.

It was quite interesting to hear all of the ideas. The players were engaged and enjoyed themselves. Each invite purchased a book and gave rave reviews about the party. One person said that it was their first experience going to a book release party and loved it. Each one invited, bought a book, told their friends, and it gained lots of sales from word of mouth.

Here's a photo of me with some of our guests.

Chapter 9

Marketing

In my research, I've seen a lot of Indie authors self-publish their book and then just let it sit there. I see a lot of complaining on forums from frustrated authors who want fast results.

I think that a writer should put the same amount of time and effort into marketing their book as they did in the creating and editing process. The way I see it, marketing is just as important as writing the book.

How are people going to know that you exist if you do not find ways to broadcast your art?

You have to believe in yourself enough to invest time and money into your masterpiece. If after you've done that and still no profit, then at least you will know what works and what doesn't. This could point you in the right direction to your true niche. That is, if your first idea didn't work out.

With services such as Amazon's KPD, it's not hard to market your book. Social media is an awesome tool as well, such as Facebook, YouTube, and Instagram, just to name a few. It takes consistency.

Here are a few options that work for me:
- Write a marketing plan that fit my situation.
- Print off marketing materials to have with me everywhere I go, such as

business cards and bookmarks.

- Sale my book at every opportunity online and in person.
- I go to events where my audience hang out both online and offline.
- Join book clubs.
- Host parties.
- Advertising and interviews via TV commercials, radio, and any other way that I can.
- I'm building my email list.
- I'm Always thinking of different ways to have fun with my marketing strategies.
- Giveaway free content.
- I like to make my book easy to buy with one click.
- I post professional photos of myself on my social media profiles.
- I make sure I give readers a way to contact me via social media or email.

- Book signings.

- Blog about my experiences as I go on my journey of writing.

The list above is just a fraction of what can be done. Each day is opportunity to try something new. Eventually it will lead to what works best for you. To me, marketing can be fun. It's just a matter of doing what fits your situation and makes you happy.

NOW GO FIND YOUR PRIVATE GETAWAY AND IMMERSE YOURSELF IN A WORLD THAT ONLY YOU CAN CREATE, AND THEN SHARE IT WITH US!

Thanks for reading! Before you go….

Here is my first, self-published Christian romance/suspense novel (Fiction-based on true story)
Fancee/ A rose amongst thorns

Volume 1   Volume 2   Volume 3

 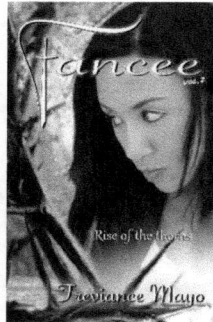 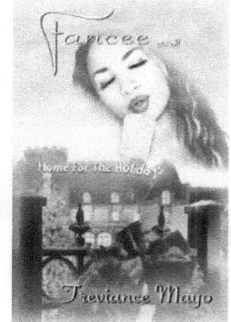

Description: Fancee is a young housewife and mother who prides herself   in her faithful relationship with her husband, Mannie Brewer. Suddenly, her marriage is turned upside down. "Mannie! You caused this! Not me!" Fancee yelled. His lip curled scornfully. His eyes flashed with a vengeful and malignant fire. His voice changed to a deceptively calm tone. "All I know is that my kids had better be home tomorrow after school. Consider yourself warned!" Fancee searches deep within herself, and spiritual beliefs to make life changing decisions. She goes through an emotional rollercoaster, and encounters a mysterious, handsome stranger along the way.

After 10 years of being published and on the shelves, I recently took this trilogy off the shelves due to something that the Lord told me to change. Perhaps I will share my story regarding why in the future. I'm being obedient to my sweet Lord and making the changes. I'm excited to republish my trilogy soon! Date to be announced to be sold at: Amazon, BarnesandNobles, iBooks,

Kobo

website: www.mayomediainc.com

ABOUT THE AUTHOR

Treviance Mayo is a lover of God the Father, God the Son our savior Jesus Christ and God the Holy Spirit. She often refers to Him as her beautiful Triune God as she is on fire for Him. She got saved at the age of 20. She is a wife, and mother of 4 children and 2 bonus children. She is multitalented; an author, film maker, videographer, screenwriter, actress, model, and singer-songwriter. She has appeared in several major films, television, music videos, fashion shows, and continues to pursue her dreams and ambitions. She is often found talking with and encouraging everyday people. She loves spending alone time with God and time with her family. Her love for writing started in 5th grade when she wrote her 1st fiction book. She is now on the quest to uplift and captivate readers worldwide, bringing them to a deeper level with God with her fiction and non-fiction books and with her family through music, and film. She quotes, "To get to really know God is to love Him! Let's go deeper and get to know Him better, together! We are HIS family!